First Light, First Water

First Light, First Water

Poems and Prose Poems by
Colin B. Douglas

Waking Lion Press

Copyright © 2014 by Colin B. Douglas. All rights reserved.
Printed in the United States of America.

ISBN 978-1-4341-0380-2

The views expressed in this book are the responsibility of the author and do not necessarily represent the position of the publisher. The reader alone is responsible for the use of any ideas or information provided by this book.

Parts of this book are works of fiction. The characters, places, and incidents in them are the products of the author's imagination or are represented fictitiously. Any resemblance of characters or events to actual persons or events is coincidental.

Published by Waking Lion Press, an imprint of The Editorium

Waking Lion Press™, the Waking Lion Press logo, and The Editorium™ are trademarks of The Editorium, LLC

The Editorium, LLC
West Jordan City, UT 84081-6132
wakinglionpress.com
wakinglion@editorium.com

Contents

Somewhere among Words — 1

A Certain Tree

Doctrine and Covenants — 5

Adonai, Forsake Me Not — 7

Adonai, I Have Sinned — 9

A Certain Tree — 11

Like a Deer He Comes to Me — 13

I Sought You, Adonai — 15

Prayer — 17

Adonai, Cover Me with Your Robe — 19

Wedding Songs — 21

Deer Come Down from the Hills — 23

A Daughter of Sarah — 25

My Beloved Shall Be Mine beyond Death — 27

Let the Stone Whisper to the Flower — 29

LET THE GRASSES SING	31
DEER HAVE PASSED HERE	33
THE EARTH UPON HER WINGS	35

LAST NIGHT'S EQUATIONS

A GIRL ON THE PLATFORM	39
A GIRL ON A BRIDGE BECKONS	41
TANGLE OF ROADS	43
I DON'T KNOW WHY THE MOON IS WHITE	45
A MIRROR HALF HIDDEN	47
LAST NIGHT'S EQUATIONS	49
A WALK IN THE WOODS	51
THE VISION OF ALL BECOMES	53
PEEL BACK A BIT OF SKIN AND SEE	55
LUMINOUS BOOKS	57
NO	59
A LONG HALLWAY	61
A MAN REMEMBERS	63
ADVENTURES OF A YOUNG MAN	65
THE BABYSITTER: A TALE OF DETECTION	75

A New Job	81
Waystation	85
There Were Several Reasons Why This Wouldn't Work	87
Still Time	89
On a Thursday	93
Banners of Past Lives	95
A Boy Sits at a Table	97
Biographical Note and Acknowledgments	99

Somewhere among Words

Somewhere among words
An opening
Search among words
As between a beloved's legs
Somewhere an opening
Somewhere light
Somewhere water
First Light
First Water

A Certain Tree

Doctrine and Covenants

Words: *matter, element, spirit, intelligence,*
Light, glory, agency, male, female, God, man.
And behind the words?
For that there is no word:
Say *I* and there is *you;*
Say *light* and there is *darkness;*
Yes and there is *no.*
It comes to this:
Sex receiving sex,
Explosion of seed,
Explosion of light, galaxies, worlds, plants, beasts,
    man and woman,
Then children, tribes, cities, wars and rumors of wars,
The cross, the empty tomb, a sea of glass;
But it comes to this:
My love, I touch your face;
Your kiss is tender.
Let us lie down in the grass.

Adonai, Forsake Me Not

Adonai, forsake me not;
Turn not away.
Sin like a girl
Comes whispering;
Like a girl with light fingers,
Whispering softly.

Adonai, I Have Sinned

Ether 3:4

Adonai, I have sinned;
I have sinned grievously against you.
My legs are water, my bowels burn;
My bowels are hot stone.
Silence encloses me like iron walls;
I cannot hear your voice.
I have sinned against you,
And your voice is shut out.
Reach forth your hand to touch me.
As you touched the small stones,
Reach forth to touch me.
Make me clean as burning stone.
I have loved you in time past;
I have embraced your fire.
Embrace me now in my uncleanness.

A Certain Tree

I am told of a certain tree
And a certain well;
That the fruit of the tree
And the water from the well
Are unspeakably sweet;
And I have tasted fruit
No man could name
And water whose source
No man could tell,
And, having tasted,
I know of greater folly
Than to seek that tree
And that well.

Like a Deer He Comes to Me

Take, eat: this is my body (Mark 14:22)

Like a deer he comes to me,
Parting the ferns,
Like a deer with bright antlers.
I chase him across meadows,
Beside streams I pursue him,
And he does not weary.
But in the thicket he surprises me,
He lets my arrow pierce him.
He gives me of his flesh at evening,
And in the bright morning
Like a deer he comes to me.

I Sought You, Adonai

I sought you, Adonai, and I found you.
I sought you among firs and alders,
Among the stars of clear skies.
I found you not there.
I sought you on hilltops,
I sought you in clear streams,
In the gold and red of trout,
And I found you not there.
But in the clouded and starless night,
When I sought you with tears,
When I knelt in ashes,
I found you; your finger touched me.
And now, among firs and alders,
Among stars and on hilltops,
In clear streams
And in the gold and red of trout,
I find you, Adonai,
I find you.

Prayer

Father, my sins are not hidden from you;
Upon my bed I remember them.
Before my shut eyes they dance
And watch me with solemn mockery.
I would forget them, Father;
Will you not remove them?
Let there be a garden of tulips before me,
Washed by spring rain;
Walk in it with me.
As a raindrop on a tulip petal,
So would I be before you.

Adonai, Cover Me with Your Robe

Adonai, cover me with your robe;
Let me rest against you.
I have traveled in far places;
Where you have sent me, I have gone.
Among serpents I have laid my bed;
I have risen to go among wolves.
I have walked in dry places
Where the rocks held no water;
I have climbed high mountains
Where frost was my covering.
I have gone unshod;
My feet have bled.
I am weary;
I have found no rest.
Let me rest against you.
Shelter me with your robe.

Wedding Songs

i

On the first morning of our marriage,
You gave me raspberries in a white bowl.
Later we stood barefoot on sand
And let white sea foam wash about our ankles.

ii

We lay down among flowers,
The grass sweet and wet,
Your dress wet.
Horses came near under blue sky,
Treading down the sweet grass,
And your dress was yellow among the flowers.

iii

The whiteness of foam,
The smell of morning rain;
And as we walked on the sand
My fingertips touched your sleeve.

iv

I come with gifts of milk and wine,
Silver shoes, and a bough of cherries,
And enter your garden of roses.

v

Your hand through the parted veil,
And later the forked flame of your thighs.
Sarai's limbs in Abram's tent
Could not have burned more bright.

Deer Come Down from the Hills

Deer come down from the hills,
Down the ravines,
Dry creek beds;
Grass dry,
Wind cold.
The high hills are colder,
Dusted by snow.
Your eyes are brown as a deer's.

A Daughter of Sarah

A daughter of Sarah is my beloved,
A priestess in Abraham's house.
Her knee is bent to the Lord;
She dwells within the circle of his law.
For virtue she is clean as the rain,
As the streams that descend the high slopes.
Her smile is as sunlight on meadows,
Her speech a sparrow's flight for gentleness.
Her counsel is heard in the congregation;
To the ears of the wise she speaks wisdom.
She gives bread to those who have not asked;
The afflicted receive comfort at her hand.
Her love she has not withheld from me;
She has given me all delights.
Sons and daughters she has given me;
Our generations will fill the heavens.
Our covenant will stand forever;
Beyond death I shall know her embrace.
Though the earth melt at his coming,
I shall never be parted from her.

My Beloved Shall Be Mine beyond Death

My beloved shall be mine beyond death,
For by His sure nails we are joined.
Though our bones go down to darkness,
I shall never be parted from her.
With the just we shall await the dawn;
In the morning we shall rise with the sun.
Our children will gather about us;
On Mount Zion we shall stand together.
In the fields of a new earth I shall embrace her;
In the gardens of a new Eden she will receive me.
Our generations will fill the heavens,
And worlds without end will honor her.

Let the Stone Whisper to the Flower

Let the stone whisper to the flower,
The flower to the sun,
And the sun to the stars of heaven,
That Jehovah is come for his bride;
She bends her knee graciously to him.
The sun hides its face,
And all silvering clouds, all shimmering snow
Are darkness to the light of her raiment.
He calls her Zion; he lifts her by the hand.
The stone whispers to the flower
And the flower to the sun
That his kiss is tender.
The table is set; the wine is served;
And the stars break forth in song.

Let the Grasses Sing

The grasses sing and the trees shout
As Shaddai descends to receive his bride.
The stones laugh and the rivers leap;
As he kisses her mouth, the clouds rain wine.
In the meadows of Eden he lies with her,
And the issue of her womb is heavenly lights.

Deer Have Passed Here

Deer have passed here,
A doe, a fawn;
Maybe a buck,
Those tracks are bigger.
They come down in moonlight
To browse on green corn.
Silent as moonlight
They pass.

The Earth upon Her Wings

The earth upon her wings moves not so quietly
As He walks in corridors of light.
Morning mists, the bloom of flowers,
Air still on meadows—
More quietly than these He goes.

Last Night's Equations

A Girl on the Platform

A girl on the platform
Hair of pearls floating on the wind
Turns slowly counterclockwise
Raises her right arm toward the sky
Hair of pearls floating
Speaks one unheard syllable
That inscribes a question on the wind

A Girl on a Bridge Beckons

A girl on a bridge beckons
A girl in a dress of broken glass
A girl with teeth of early snow
A girl whose legs are marble pillars on a distant hill
A girl with hair of ivy where small birds nest
A girl whose eyes are open doorways
A girl who knows what is written behind the mirror

Tangle of Roads

Tangle of roads, houses, seas
Tangle of hallways and doors and glass
A face beyond the tangled highways of the sun
Of seas and rocks and shoals and shores

I Don't Know Why the Moon Is White

I don't know why the moon is white
I don't know where the butterflies sleep
I don't know why a man leans a ladder against a wall
Or why the wall curves gently away

A Mirror Half Hidden

A mirror half hidden by fallen leaves
White hand extended through the glass
Deer pass through the clearing one by one
And do not leave a scrap of paper to blow
Across the grass in a hot wind
Beneath a white sun obscured by antlers
Eyes unblinking in the glare
We watch from behind a corner of a distant building
And wait to fall into the mirror

Last Night's Equations

Last night's equations are inscribed on the eyes of morning
A woman holds in her teeth the moon
As delicately as Urim balanced on the tip of a salmon's fin
The moon slips from the woman's teeth
The eyes of morning take its place
The equations float
White feathers back into the night

A Walk in the Woods

A walk in the woods
Leaves brown and golden
Golden towers rising above the trees
Girls on the lake shore
Naked, watchful,
Eyes of red stoplights
Swinging in the wind on a single cable
Storm rising in the east
Rain washing the towers
Plastic blowing in the wind
Wraps about the girls

The Vision of All Becomes

The vision of all becomes
As a face peering through leaves
Expressionless
Wordless
A tangle of branches and leaves
Behind them a mirror set against a tree trunk
And in the mirror a face
The trees veiled in snow
Ecstatic beneath the sun

Peel Back a Bit of Skin and See

Peel back a bit of skin and see
The sun blazing over stone and sand
And rivulets of light
Trickling through the crevices of fear

Luminous Books

Luminous books
A pool of goldfish flaming
Snow rising through the grass
What is this book that speaks
Of snow and goldfish and grass

No

No memory
No feet
No eyes
No light
No darkness
No pendants flapping in the breeze
No yellow pendants
No blue pendants
No red pendants
No face looking up from beneath the surface of the water
No lovers enfolded among the ferns
No book lying open beneath the sun
No voice

A Long Hallway

A long hallway, old wallpaper, old carpet, musty smell, bare dim lightbulbs hanging by cords from the ceiling, yellowed white-painted doors, many doors both sides of the hallway, the hallway not straight; it curves gradually to the right, the line of sight cut off in the distance just before the the lines converge. Whether the hallway makes a circle, that remains unanswered, but open a door and then another: behind one a lilac grove, behind another an empty room, behind another a boulevard by the sea, and one's greatest desire, after all, is to lie down by the sea and sleep.

A Man Remembers

A man remembers a house in a small town, in a country of firs and much rain. He awakes one night to the sound of rain on the roof, and unable to return to sleep he rises from his bed and goes to the back door to watch the rain fall. In a puddle near the door a pale plastic doll lies naked, face up. He is alone in this house, there are no children, and he wonders how the doll has come to be there. There was a woman in this house the night before. He stood with her in the kitchen, kissing her mouth, his right hand lifting the hem of her dress. The doll is more pink than the skin of that woman. Near the house is an apple orchard, old and neglected, the trees overgrown, apples rotting on the ground. He likes the smell of the rotting apples in the fall. Beyond the orchard stand large old fir trees, and among the trees a house, white, two-storied. There are children there, but there is no reason why any of them should have been in his back yard, leaving a naked doll on the ground.

Adventures of a Young Man

He awoke in the dark in the earliest hours of the third day in a cheap hotel room to see, standing at the foot of his bed, the faint image of a young woman in a blue hooded cloak. She said, "Come, follow me; it is time." She turned and walked toward the door, and he arose, already dressed, and followed her out the door, leaving the door open and nothing behind him.

He followed her down the hallway, a narrow passage with yellow walls and a thin carpet of uncertain gray to brown, lighted at each end by a bare bulb hanging by a strand of electrical cord. Standing at one doorway with a hand on the knob was a man in red, at another a man in yellow, at a third a man in white; none of them looked at him as he passed, just stared at the floor as if trying to recall something.

He followed the woman down the stairway at the end of the hall, winding down three floors, out into the lobby and past the desk clerk, who was asleep in his chair behind an iron grill, out onto the dark street, where she turned to the right and proceeded down the sidewalk.

The street was deserted, except for the three men: the man in red stood beneath a lamppost with his head and shoulders slightly bowed and his arms extended and hands apart as if holding a large package; the man in yellow stood at attention in the intersection ahead; the man in white stood inside the entryway of a shop that dealt in curios from small and poor South American nations—blowguns; shrunken heads of Guaraní children; small refrigerators with missing doors; dresses worn by female impersonators who had performed in mediocre tourist hotels of the twenties and thirties; a piece of damp, dark cloth with a slightly sour smell. (He had seen all of this when he visited the store in his childhood; once with his father; several times, he thought, with his mother and her sisters. He had been in the store once at a time when it sold supplies and paraphernalia for spiritist rituals: table after table loaded with dusty tangles of herbs and grasses; candles; bottles of powdered viscera of bats and coral snakes; complete human skins stripped in the twinkling of an eye from unsuspecting office workers as they waited at bus stops and elevators; Haitian cigarettes in tin boxes; a profusion of small baskets and boxes woven of various natural fibers; small objects that he saw out of the corners of his eyes but was unable to bring into focus sufficiently long to identify them; and wild violets, jeweled with dew, pressing up everywhere through the endless piles of merchandise. Once, inside the shop, as he stood among the tables, he became vaguely anxious, fearful of being recognized as an enemy, and, looking about for a place to hide, he spied a large object of red glass and slipped behind it. As he looked through the thin and quite transparent glass, he gradually realized that this was a sculpture of a vulva, and he was standing within the curve of the concave side.)

Then they turned a corner and were standing before an immense and ancient mansion, which he had never before noticed but which he recognized had been there long before the city that surrounded it had been conceived. It was many stories high, though he didn't count. There were turrets and battlements and ledges, and windows of the deepest black; gargoyles and the Green Man everywhere; cornucopiae spilling fruits and sheaves of grain; and carved along the faces of the ledges runes and glyphs and formulae and outlines of continents and scenes of love and hunting and battle. It was all in wine-red brick, in some places crumbling to dust that floated out onto the night air and fell slowly and silently toward the street: immensity and darkness looming against the stars; hovering doves; the possibility of a great forest within. The air bled.

The mansion was surrounded by a stone wall surmounted by a spiked iron fence. They stood before a gate that curved high above them, and the woman said: "This is the house of which you have been told. You have choices, which are both few and many. Find the box containing the Urim and Thummim, and hope that you will remember their use. Take this ring, on which you see carved in bdellium the last letter of the alphabet of the angels. Now, go."

He climbed seventy steps to the door. Upon entering, he found myself in a large foyer, the floor of which was cluttered with various computer-like machines and instruments, which he recognized as belonging to a French organization for the study of paranormal phenomena. To his right was another door into what appeared to be a receptionist's room. Behind the receptionist's desk sat a young man, Somalian, he thought, of urbane demeanor. He approached the young man and stood before his desk. The man looked up and said: "Good morning, sir. I will be with you momentarily."

He punched two keys on his computer, adjusted a thin stack of papers, and returned his attention to his visitor.

"How may I help you, sir?"

Without speaking, the visitor held the ring out to him. He took it, examined it, and said, "I see. Well."

The receptionist handed back the ring and sat back in his chair and folded his hands on the desktop.

"We have been waiting for you for some time. Some of us were beginning to lose hope. Are you ready?"

"I suppose so. There was nowhere else to go."

"What instructions have you received?"

"'This is the house of which you have been told. You have choices, which are both few and many. Find the box containing the Urim and Thummim, and hope that you will remember their use. Take this ring, on which you see carved in bdellium the last letter of the alphabet of the angels. Now, go.'"

"That's not much to go on, is it?"

"No, I suppose not."

"Well, let me show you to the entrance. Whether you go on or not is, of course, up to you, though we do have our reasons for hoping that you will."

The receptionist arose and took the visitor back out to the foyer. At the rear of the foyer was a doorway the visitor hadn't noticed when he first came in. The casing was plain and white, like that of a bedroom or a closet of an ordinary house. The door itself was missing, though the brass hinges were still in place. An unlighted staircase rose from just within the door. The steps were of bare wood, and worn.

"We haven't picked up any movement here for several months. That's all I can tell you."

The visitor stood in the doorway and looked up the stairs. They disappeared into complete darkness about twenty steps up.

"All right," he said. "Thank you."

He climbed for a long time in the darkness. For a time he could see the bright rectangle of the door below when he looked back, but then it disappeared. He supposed the stairway had turned slightly in one direction or the other, though he hadn't noticed which.

He came to what seemed to be a landing. Feeling about, he found a door knob and turned it. The door opened inward into a hallway. He stepped inside and shut the door behind him. He followed the hallway until it turned to the right, and he was standing inside a simple bedroom. A young woman—sandy-colored hair, a light gray sweatshirt, blue denim jeans—was making the bed. She flipped out the white sheet, let it settle, then worked around the bed tucking the edges under the mattress. She made hospital corners. She laid out the second sheet and tucked it under and made hospital corners at the foot. She laid out a quilt and a spread, folded them back, put pillows in place, and then tucked the bedding around them.

"The children are outside," she said. "I will call them for lunch in a few minutes."

She left the room, and he followed her.

The house was small. There was a small hallway from which two bedrooms and a bathroom opened. The hallway opened into a living room, which was spacious for the size of the house. One door of the room opened directly outside; the other into the kitchen. This was a wooden frame house. The floors were wood, and the varnish had mostly worn off. The living room floor was partially covered by a large worn rug of the same material as the carpet in the hallway of the hotel.

The kitchen door stood open. It was a warm, sunny day. There was a screen door, and he stood at the kitchen door looking out through the screen. There was a yard with grass, a high wooden fence around the yard, big leafy trees outside the fence all around the yard. There were blue sky and white clouds, the sound of bees, the drone of an airplane, the sound of hammering.

The woman opened the refrigerator and took out a glass bottle of milk and a package of baloney. She set them on the counter. She took a loaf of Wonderbread in its white wrapper with red, blue, and yellow polka dots from a bread box and set it on the counter. She made a baloney sandwich and cut it in half and put the halves on separate plates. She made a peanut butter and blackberry jam sandwich and cut it and put the halves on the plates. She put a few potato chips on each plate. She poured milk into two glasses. She set everything on the table, a Formica table with chromed legs, and vinyl and chrome chairs.

He was standing on the grass near the fence when she called the children. There was a smell of hot wood, the children frozen in the motions of going into the house, a bird frozen in the air just above the fence. A miniature of the glass vulva rested on a white embroidered cloth on the chest of drawers. A drawer slid open. As he reached out to touch the denim over her knee, she lay back, a mound of yellow sweet-smelling flowers in the sun, as one wall of the bedroom was no longer there. Always, it had been like this. He walked away with a pang of disappointment to look for the second door, down the long hallway, past the man in red (where were the yellow and the white?), back into the stairwell, groping about in the darkness, finding the stairs upward, climbing again into the darkness.

The second door. Another hallway, along each side stalls from which, as he passed, men and women performing a variety of erotic acts, most of which he thought he would not have enjoyed but some of which intrigued him, looked up at him with hostile eyes. He came to one stall that, unlike the others, was hidden by a partition. In the partition was a door on which was painted in black the last letter of the alphabet of the angels. He opened the door and found the stall empty, except for a high four-legged stool on which sat an ornately carved cedar box. He opened the box and found within it two crystal spheres the size of large marbles. He picked them up and examined them. He could not remember their use. He replaced them in the box and set the box on the stool and turned his attention to the walls of the stall.

They were completely covered with pictures of varying sizes. The largest were about the size of his hand, the smallest the size of the nail of one of his little fingers. He focused on one chosen at random. There was the girl in the blue cloak standing at a table in the spiritist shop holding in her hand and closely examining a two-pronged object that he couldn't make out, though it looked similar to the one he remembered having seen in the curio shop. He turned to another and saw the man in yellow holding a bunch of blue flowers resembling the wild violets he had seen growing in the curio shop. In another he saw the sandy-haired woman from the first door walking the hallway that led from the door into her house. The picture caught her midstep. Her back was to him, and in the foreground of the picture was a large, dark figure that seemed to be following her. The figure's back also was turned to him, and he could not make out whether it was human or something else. Hanging from a nail on one wall of the hallway, somewhat ahead of the woman, was what appeared to be a white garment, and, just beyond the garment, a door. How had he overlooked that door before? On the door was the numeral 3 in brass. He would have to retrace his steps.

He turned to where the door of the stall had been, and it was no longer there. He looked all about him. There was no door anywhere. He also noticed that there seemed to be no source of light in the room, yet he could see with perfect clarity. He found the picture of the girl in the blue cloak standing in the spiritist shop, but she had moved. She had turned away from the table, and her hand was reaching behind her to replace the two-pronged object. In the distance, unnoticed by the girl, the man in red, the man in yellow, and the man in white stood together, looking toward her. One of them held before himself a picture frame about two feet square, and within the frame, in black on a white background, was a single glyph: the last letter of the alphabet of the angels.

There were the letter, the ring, the two crystal spheres in the cedar box. Where was the door?

He reached into the picture and took hold of the letter with both hands, gripping it like the steering wheel of a cream-colored Desoto he once had driven down a country road in summer under a canopy of great leafy trees. He had been just previously lying in a field beyond the trees in a bed of yellow flowers, their heavy perfume rising like steam under the steady sun. What was her name? *Legion,* he was sure. He grasped the letter with both hands, but it refused to move. He let it go and returned to the cedar box. He opened it, removed the crystal spheres, and held them to his eyes. The receptionist sat before him behind his counter.

"Congratulations, sir," the receptionist said. "I see you are beginning to recall their use. Your choices have been many, but you have recognized few of them. This is the common experience of men. Her name was Legion, as you remembered. But fear not; I am with you always."

The vision closed, and he was alone again in the stall. He returned the spheres to the box and put the box in a pocket of his jacket. He went to the wall through which he had entered, thrust his hands into it, and tore it. He stepped through into the hallway and walked back in the direction from which he had come. The hostile inhabitants of the stalls were gone now, and scraps of yellowed newspaper blew in the wind across darkened streets. He went back through the second door and felt his way down the stairs to the first and went back through it. He brushed past the dark, hulking figure without discerning its identity, past the sandy-haired woman who was frozen midstep, past the white garment hanging from the nail, to the door to which was riveted the brass figure of the numeral 3, opened the door, and went through.

He was standing in a field of grass under a summer sun. The air was warm. At a short distance were the man in red, the man in yellow, the man in white; the first standing erect and looking toward the sun, the second crouching as if to kneel, the third on his knees with his face in his hands. To the right of them was the girl in the blue cloak, holding the two-pronged object in her hands with her head bowed, as if presenting it as an offering to a sacred image. To the right of her, the receptionist sat behind his desk, absorbed in a sheaf of papers. To the right of him the woman whose name was Legion stood on a mound of yellow flowers. Her jeans were cut away to expose her privates, and two holes were cut in her sweatshirt to expose her breasts. Behind him, he knew without looking, was the road that passed under the canopy of trees, and the cream-colored Desoto moving along the road.

"Now we are making progress," he said aloud. He walked up to each of the figures in turn. Each was made of cardboard, supported by a flimsy wooden frame. They reminded him of a dream he had had as child, of giraffes standing about on a hillside, each made of cardboard supported by a wooden frame. He pushed each figure over in turn with a touch of his hand. They lay in the grass in the sunshine, and he stood with his hands clasped behind his back, gazing across the prairie, waiting for the last letter of the alphabet of the angels to appear above the horizon.

The Babysitter: A Tale of Detection

i.

The call from my partner, Dobson, comes shortly after midnight. "I don't want to spoil the surprise," Dobson says. "You gotta see this for yourself."

It's in a lower middle-class neighborhood, nice houses, nothing special. This house is white, two stories, old. The crime scene is set up when I get there—flashing lights, yellow tape, uniforms everywhere. Dobson stands on the front porch.

"What's happening?" I ask him.

He shakes his head. "Nothing like I've ever seen," he says, "and I thought I'd seen it all."

I follow him through the front door. He touches the shoulder of one of the two uniforms who are standing in front of us, and they make way, and there's Mrs. Brineholt sitting on the living room sofa in red pants and top, rocking back and forth, holding the baby's head to her chest. Just the head. The body is nowhere in sight.

"Jesus, Mary, and Joseph," I say. "What is this?"

Dobson shakes his head again. "As far as we can figure out, they came home from a movie about eleven-thirty. The babysitter was gone, and the baby's head was sitting on the coffee table. We haven't found the body. A neighbor heard the screaming and called nine-one-one. By the time the first car got here, she was sitting like this, in shock. She won't let us take it away from her, and she won't communicate. There's an ambulance and a shrink on the way. We haven't found the babysitter, either."

"Where's the husband?"

"In the kitchen, looking pretty much like her. There's a uniform with him, too. Come on upstairs. You need to see the baby's room."

I follow him up the stairs.

The room is all pastel pink and yellow and white and blue, very clean and tidy, except for the crib and the floor around it. Evidently the baby was killed in the crib. The blankets are soaked with dark, clotted blood. It has puddled on the plastic mattress cover underneath and trickled down the side at one corner onto the floor.

"The killer must have put the body in some kind of a container, maybe a plastic bag, before he left the crib, because there's not a trace of blood anywhere else in the house. Must have put the head in a bag, too, to take it downstairs."

We go back downstairs. The lab boys are dusting for prints, cameras are flashing, the ambulance has arrived, and the shrink with a hypodermic needle to sedate the Brineholts, who are carried out on stretchers. The medical examiner puts the head in a plastic bag and puts that in a brown paper bag and takes it to the morgue. I give orders for armed guards to be put on the front and back doors twenty-four hours a day until further notice and go home to bed for four more hours.

Morning, Dobson and I are both at the precinct early. He's there first. I pull up a chair close to his desk and say,

"Show me what we've got." He takes from a drawer of his desk a brown paper bag much like the one the medical examiner used a few hours ago, which he sets carefully on the desk top. The top of the bag is rolled. He unrolls it deliberately, then reaches inside and takes out and sets on the desk—at this point, memory fails me—either three highly polished silver balls, the size of large marbles, or one grossly pornographic postcard addressed "To whom it may concern."

ii.

In the darkness just before dawn a young woman carrying a white plastic trash bag loaded with a heavy, bulky object approaches a gate in a wall. The wall is made of cinder blocks and is more than eight feet high. The gate is of iron. It has no handle on the outside, only a small square hole covered on the inside. The young woman approaches the gate across a deserted street, looking nervously from side to side.

The gate is set inside the wall about two feet, and the entryway thus formed is darkly shadowed. The young woman steps into the darkness and raps three times on the gate with a small mallot she finds hanging there. The window opens immediately and a stern voice says, "What do you want?" The face behind the voice is invisible in the darkness.

"I'm the babysitter," the young woman whispers. "I've come to deliver the package and get new instructions."

The window cover slams shut with a metallic clink, and the gate begins to open inward, slowly and silently.

The young woman stands holding the white bag at her left side. She is very patient. Before the door has fully opened, the night, a day, and most of another night pass.

Meanwhile, flowers from the gardens within the wall slip silently through the opening—hyacinth, iris, snapdragon, yellow daisy, orchid, tulip, daffodil, certain species of Campanula, the entire order Rubiales, one by one, like the notes of a lesser known étude of Chopin played very slowly, and join the procession passing on the street behind her.

This procession has its origin in a distant part of the city, where the players' costumes are manufactured in vile sweatshops, situated at appropriate intervals on the banks of rivers, the confluence of which escapes the attention of most cartographers, however appreciative they might be of Chopin, of the craftsmanly murder of infants, of Rubiales, even of the more subtle varieties of alibi concocted by the most desperate criminals.

The procession passes this point on the street at almost the exact same time each morning, though sometimes later. The young woman knows nothing of this, of course, and only considers herself fortunate to witness so artful a display, which she watches by a kind of second sight without having to turn away from the gate. She remains in her place until the last wagon has passed, and her left leg becomes indistinguishable from those of the ivory statues on display in the quarters of the tailors who made the costumes, and the ivy creeps furtively up her inner thigh. The liberties taken by the ivy signal the moment for her to enter the garden.

iii.

We conduct the interrogation on a tiled area near the fountain. We sit at a small table, the babysitter across from me, Dobson at my left. I place on the table a life-sized Latex model of the body of the infant as we imagine it must have looked in reality, while still intact.

"What do you know about this?" I ask.

"Who are you?" she asks. "Are you here to give me my new instructions?"

Dobson smirks. "Oh, we'll give you instructions, all right."

"What's in the bag?" I ask her, trying to ignore Dobson.

"I think I want to talk to an attorney," she says.

"Oh, we'll get you an attorney all right," Dobson says, continuing to smirk.

"If you won't give me new instructions, then I must show my attorney this," she says, pulling the hem of her dress far up on her left thigh. The leg is completely, thickly enveloped in ivy, almost to the top. My eyes are fixed on the two inches of snowy flesh between the edge of her dress and the top of the ivy. She extends the leg out to the side until her heel rests several yards away in a patch of hyacinth that has failed to escape with its fellows.

I begin to fear that the case is insoluble, and I arise and walk slowly and sadly out to find the procession, leaving Dobson to his own devices.

iv.

I enter a small restaurant at noontime, not really expecting to find a seat open, but there is Dobson sitting at the counter with an empty seat at his left. Sitting on the counter in front of him, just beyond his plate, in fact, is the head, still showing not a sign of decomposition. I still marvel at how cleanly it has been cut off, so that it sits there on the stump of the neck as evenly and firmly as a bust of Pythagoras.

I haven't thought of Pythagoras in years.

I sit down beside Dobson.

"Well," I say, "any progress?"

"Plenty," he says. "You left too soon."

"Did she confess?"

"No. She's still holding out. But we expect her to crack any day now."

The head is beginning to undergo a transformation. It grows larger, and the angelic infant features are maturing, grossening. I order a toasted ham and cheese sandwich and watch the transformation progress while I wait. Dobson has already finished his lunch—a double cheeseburger with fries—and is drinking his coffee, holding the cup in two hands with his elbows resting on the counter, looking glumly down at the head. By this time it is that of a large, fat, and bald adult, rather resembling an older Mussolini.

"It keeps doing this," Dobson says. "Last time it was Charles Manson. The time before that it was some old Greek."

"Pythagoras," I say, instantly knowing.

"Yeah, him. How'd you know?"

I have no answer. I am lost in a memory of standing on a beach a long time ago, something like Miami Beach, looking at a lifeguard's tower, where the girl sits holding a baby, and ivy is growing up all about the tower, and from the tower in each direction along the beach as far as I can see is a line of busts of Pythagoras, carved in ivory, sitting in the sand and looking toward the sea.

A New Job

"We'll start you in the Receiving Department."
   I am truly grateful for the job.
   "Take this paper through that door and give it to Sheryl. She'll tell you what to do."
   I take the paper through the indicated door and find myself in an enormous open bay of desks where young men work at computer terminals. Line upon line of desks, lines so long I can't see the end of them. Fluorescent lighting, beige and gray walls and floor, acoustical tile ceiling—your standard modern office, but so many desks.
   A young woman sits at a counter to my right. I give her the paper and say, "I'm looking for Sheryl."
   "Of course you are," she says, "and you should be truly grateful for the job."
   She takes the paper and starts down the aisle between two lines of desks. She pauses to speak to someone, pauses as if to think, turns, pauses, continues on, working her way down the aisle, her dress a patch of blue here, there, moving down the aisle, becoming very small. Then I see that the far end of the office bay is a forest of pines. The blue patch moves into the forest and disappears among the trees.
   Standing among the trees, sunlight filtering through the boughs and needles. Before me a building, like a warehouse, one story, concrete and steel, surrounded by a chain link

fence with no gate in sight. Over the door a sign: "Receiving Department." The door opens inward, and a young woman steps out wearing blue denims, western boots, a white cotton shirt with the tails tied up to expose a lean abdomen. She leans against the wall to one side of the door with her right elbow resting in her left hand, holding a cigarette on which she draws from time to time. I standing watching her for a long time, wondering if this is Sheryl. All the time I watch her, the sun hardly seems to move.

"Come in," she says eventually, between draws on the cigarette.

There is still no way in, so I go to the right, along the fence line, which turns to my left. I follow the fence to the left until I realize it extends beyond my sight into the forest. I stop and turn to look behind me and see it also extends out of sight the way I've just come. I wonder what to do. The sun is warm through the trees, the pines smell hot, and finally I am so overcome by sleepiness I lie down on the carpet of red, brittle pine needles and sleep.

In a hotel room, looking through the window toward a beach in late afternoon. The shadows are long. At the edge of the beach, silhouetted against the restless water, six giraffes are blazing furiously, great orange and yellow fires.

"I'm looking for. . . ." and I stop, not knowing how to finish the sentence. I am speaking to a young woman who stands behind me, to my right. I can't see her, but it is impossible to be unaware of her presence.

"I know," she says, "but I can't help you without more information. So I suggest we stick to questions that can be answered, like 'how long can this go on?' "

The giraffes, who are all standing, writhe and contort, flinging up one leg, then another. Their mouths are open in silent screams. Indeed, how long?

A wind is up, and pennants flutter, blue and yellow. On each is embroidered in white block letters a word of which I can make out only "RY."

Waystation

A small house at the edge of a cliff overlooks a sea. The one door and all the windows have long since been removed by scavengers, but the scavengers are not vandals, and they have left undamaged the true treasure contained within this house: the pictures. The pictures cover the walls and ceilings; the door frames; the cupboards, inside and out; every inch of paintable surface is covered with them. There are undoubtedly many thousands of them, though no one is known to have counted. Some have begun but after several days have recognized the hopelessness of the task. One investigator found that some of the pictures moved to other locations even as he counted them. The pictures are of all sizes, some as large as the stretch of a man's arms and some so small that even with a magnifying glass one can barely make out the scenes depicted. The windows at the back of the house overlook the sea, and as seen through one of the windows the view is always sunlit, the sky always blue, the sea always blue and white-capped, no matter what the time of day or the weather or light conditions as seen from outside. At times the wind sweeps rain throughout the house, but the pictures are miraculously undamaged. The colors have never faded and in some cases seem actually to have brightened with the passing of years. Once as I stood in the kitchen, looking out toward the sea, I was certain that a woman sat at the table behind me, drinking tea and turning the pages of a volume of verse, but I understood that if I turned she would not be there, so I continued looking out the window. The air was laden with a scent of mowed grass warming in summer sunlight. Later I found a picture of her, about as large as the palm of my hand, sitting at that very table with the very cup of tea and a book, but she was turned slightly away from me, and I couldn't see her face. Beside that picture was another of a man walking along a road bordered on either side by a stone wall overgrown with a profusion of roses. He wore a broad-brimmed hat of the kind seen in pictures of the young Goethe and carried a staff, and he appeared to be moving at a leisurely pace beneath the summer sun. I recognized that road; it passed a mere mile from the cliff's edge. So far as I know I have never met the man himself, although I have sometimes remembered that I myself was the man. I sometimes remember walking leisurely along that road, raising dust in the motionless air, knowing I was approaching the lane that turned toward the house. I don't remember having actually arrived at the house on that journey, and often I remember nothing of the journey at all.

There Were Several Reasons Why This Wouldn't Work

There were several reasons why this wouldn't work. For one, the road extended indefinitely beyond the horizon, down a narrow hallway papered in yellow and hung with the ivory arms of lost infants. For another, a mirror hung in the air in innumerable particles of glittering dust, remembering vaguely its old place on the wall of a small house in the woods, or peering out from among the clotted roots of cedars and spruces. I have tried to explain this, but you know how it was: money was scarce, the weather uncertain, the smell of the spruces under the hot sun heavy in the air. Then the children came, a procession of them, so many, shuffling silently along the yellow corridor, eyes wide and soft and sad, thinking of earlier days when they conversed freely with deer whose antlers were bright with rain. We lay on our bed, propped on our elbows, watching them, hardly conscious of our nakedness, remembering light on ancient seas.

Still Time

A man was watching the movements of a yellow snake as thick as his wrist and as long as he was tall. He stood on a strip of broken, weed-grown asphalt, holding a baby cradled in his left arm, with his right hand supporting, the baby loosely wrapped in a pastel blue cotton blanket with a corner laid over its face to protect it from the sun. The heat was becoming oppressive. He smelled the asphalt, and the weeds were drooping.

Rising up from the old asphalt road was an embankment of granite stones the size of the baby's head, an embankment as massive as the face of a great dam. At the top of the embankment, out of sight, beyond the upper edge, was the highway. The baby's mother, who had been the man's wife, was waiting there, sitting on the shoulder of the highway with her back against the protective barrier. Her back was turned to him; he knew that.

He knew that this country had no venomous snakes; he had heard that; all of his life he had believed that; he remembered that; and he thought of it as he watched the sinuous tube of yellow emerge from the stones a few yards up the embankment and disappear again among stones a few yards away. There must be mice living under the stones, he thought. He felt the heat around him rise by degrees. If he did not begin climbing the embankment right away, he would need to find shade, and there was some below the asphalt road, under the trees that grew along a trickle of creek. He could rest there for awhile.

But he did not. He began to pick his way carefully up the stony slope. The tips of thistle leaves emerged tentatively between stones ahead of him. Where there are thistles there may be the yellow snakes, he remembered. He picked his way carefully. The baby beside him held the little finger of his left hand and tried to keep up, but the man knew that it was difficult for him. The asphalt road behind him was becoming crowded with trailer trucks, the great blue boxes rattling their sides together, and he wondered if the woman would wait for him. A snake lept from between two stones toward his face, and he batted it away with his right hand, startled.

He remembered the first time he had seen one of these yellow snakes. It was a long time ago, when he was a boy.

How had he come to be at the bottom of this embankment, standing alongside this broken piece of the old, two-lane highway? He did not remember, though he supposed that he must have come over the hills behind him. He had come from somewhere beyond those hills. A fragmentary memory came to him of carrying the infant through a tangle of tall grass, in the heat of an early August afternoon, watching large yellow snakes as thick as his own thigh squirm slowly away from his careful, slow steps.

He turned to his left to find his former wife standing beside him, knowing that she simultaneously was sitting with her back against the protective barrier above him, and he said to her, "I'll try to get to you in time. I'll try to get to you before they come. Please wait for me."

"I'll be there," she replied. "There is still time."

And then he was alone. He wondered if it would be easier to drop down across the road and into the ravine. He did so, and standing in the creek in the bottom of the ravine he grabbed at a fish with both hands, but it slipped away into the reeds; and he looked back up the slope to the highway above, and the woman, now with his own face, and a yellow snake coiled on her lap, looked up and said, "I will wait. There is still time."

On a Thursday

I last saw her on a midafternoon in late June, unseasonably cool, and I was eating a sandwich at a food court in a shopping mall. It was a Thursday. I was alone at a table against a wall, and I saw her walking quickly along the opposite side. She was wearing a white dress printed with small red flowers and a pale blue sweater, and carrying a white purse hanging from her left shoulder. Her hair was cut shorter than usual, but still blonde, held back from her ears by red barettes. It flounced a bit as she walked, quickly, intently, looking directly forward, not turning her head, and she didn't see me.

The instant I saw her I put down my sandwich and went after her. I called her name, but she seemed to pay no attention, just kept walking. I dodged between the tables as politely as I could, but I couldn't reach her before she turned the corner into the mall concourse. I turned after her and walked fast, careful not to collide with people but hurrying. She kept walking, and I kept following, but I couldn't catch her. She exited the mall by the south exit and continued down the sidewalk. I followed, but I couldn't seem to move fast enough. We walked on and on, out of the city center, into a rundown section of pawnshops and sandwich counters and adult bookstores and parking garages, then car lots and a Blue Boutique, the Southern Xposure Club for Members Only, then more car lots. We came to where weeds grew up through cracks in the sidewalk, then a vacant lot, then warehouses and wholesale dealers. I was nearly a block behind her when she suddenly cut across the street—a deserted street—and went through the door of a large, high, windowless and nameless building. I followed her across and through the door, and I was in a large open bay filled with desks and computer terminals and keyboard operators. The ceiling was high, and the bay was lighted by bright fluorescent lamps. She walked down an aisle between desks, and I followed behind, and she went through a door at the back of the room, and I followed, and as I passed through the door I saw as in a vision the immensity of the place, buildings and parking lots and more buildings, and she was out there somewhere, and I walked on, frantically, desiring to smell her perfume on that blue sweater and feel its softness against my face again.

Banners of Past Lives

We departed early, raising banners of past lives before us. The road lay through a run-down subdivision on the edge of the city, a place where housewives still hung clothes on lines to dry. One wore a dark blue dress with a low hem and long sleeves, and a light-blue bandana around her head and a white apron. She kept the clothespins in a large pocket on the apron. Her husband, who had lost an arm in combat, sat inside in the breakfast nook reading a newspaper and drinking lukewarm coffee. It was necessary for him to lay down the paper each time he wanted to pick up his cup. (They still made love, however, usually in the woman-astride position, though occasionally in the "crayfish.") When he heard the commotion raised by our passing, the husband came to the doorway to watch, wearing the expression of a man remembering a past life, a life of gallantry and glory in long-past wars in that southern country where the housewives are often trapped in the walls, moving about silently in the dark spaces.

We were tired. The previous night we had ascended and descended stairways endlessly, remaining resolutely cheerful, but tired. We always were tempted to open one of the doors that we occasionally passed on the stairways, hoping to find a comfortable place to lie down, but rest came rarely to us—it was necessary to keep moving as long as possible, though there was no actual requirement, only a sense of inescapable duty. We therefore departed early, raising the banners of past lives.

At a rest stop, we sat at picnic tables in the shade of cottonwood trees and watched the travelers stroll on the grass and consider their plans. The place was infested with snakes, mottled red snakes about twelve inches long. They were being called "coral snakes," though I knew that was incorrect. They had short, needle-sharp teeth and the ability to leap into the air fully extended, the tip of the tail attaining to one or two inches above the ground. They caused much apprehension, but there was reason to believe that they were not venomous. A young man whom I knew to be somewhat impulsive in his behavior was playing with one of them, teasing it, pulling at its tail, holding it and shifting it from hand to hand. "I hope you will let that go," I said to him, and he replied, "I want to do this." The previous night, I had passed him on the stairs, and it had occurred to me then that he might be troublesome.

A Boy Sits at a Table

A boy sits at a table in an immense library filled with shelves of large and heavy books. In the books are all the secrets that forever draw us on and forever elude us. Before him on the table is a book open and inviting him to read, and he does read, but afterward he remembers only fragments of sentences, even of words: "the key that unlocks the door of," "ington has painted," "ewise," "a girl's shoe lying in the hallway."

Biographical Note and Acknowledgments

Colin Blaine Douglas was born in 1944 and brought up in Western Washington; is an enrolled member of the Samish Indian Nation; became a Latter-day Saint at the age of sixteen; served in the Brazilian Mission in 1964–1966; served in Military Intelligence in the Regular Army and the Utah National Guard, retiring as a sergeant first class; attended the University of Washington as a journalism major and received a bachelor's degree in psychology and a master's degree in American literature at Brigham Young University; was employed for twenty years as an editor in the Curriculum Department of The Church of Jesus Christ of Latter-day Saints; edited and reported for the *Magna* (Utah) *Times* newspaper for two years; with the former Linda Jean Wells, to whom he was married in 1969, is the father of seven; has resided in Utah since 1971; as literary favorites names Latter-day Saint scripture (including the Bible), Arthur Rimbaud, André Breton, Ezra Pound, T. S. Eliot, Kenneth Rexroth, Gary Snyder, and Philip Lamantia.

"I sought you, Adonai," *Ensign*, Oct. 1979
"Let the stone whisper to the flower," *Dialogue* 13.4 (1980)
"Like a deer he comes to me," *Dialogue* 13.4 (1980); *Harvest: Contemporary Mormon Poems,* ed. Eugene England and Dennis Clark (Salt Lake City: Signature Books, 1989)
"My beloved shall be mine beyond death," *Ensign*, Feb. 1981

"A daughter of Sarah is my beloved," *Sunstone* 8.6 (1983)
"Adonai: cover me with your robe," *Sunstone* 10.10 (1986); *Harvest* (1989)
"Wedding songs," *Sunstone* 10.10 (1986); *Harvest* (1989)
"Let the grasses sing," *Sunstone* 10.10 (1986)
"Adonai: I have sinned" and "Adonai: forsake me not," *Sunstone* 12.1 (1988)
"Prayer," *Irreantum*, 2006

www.ingramcontent.com/pod-product-compliance
Lightning Source LLC
Chambersburg PA
CBHW022116090426
42743CB00008B/873